I SPY
TWO EYES

— Numbers In Art —

For Walter and Molly

F O R E W O R D

When my own children were tiny, they loved looking at the pictures in a book of medieval paintings. They were fascinated by the minute details and the rich colors and patterns. Over the years we have looked at hundreds of pictures from all over the world, and I hope you will enjoy the twenty I have chosen for this book. They are all paintings except for one, which is a beautiful Japanese woodblock print.

I dedicate this book to my children, without whom I would never have thought of it.

Lucy Micklethwait, 1992

I SPY
TWO EYES

Numbers In Art

Devised & selected by Lucy Micklethwait

Greenwillow Books, New York

I spy
one fly

1

Swabian School, *Portrait of a Woman of the Hofer Family*

GEBORNE HOFERIN·

I spy
two eyes

Karel Appel, *Cry for Freedom*

I spy
three puppies

3

Paul Gauguin, *Still Life with Three Puppies* (1888)

I spy
four fish

Henri Matisse, *Goldfish*

I spy
five eggs

Jan van Huijsum, *Flowers in a Terracotta Vase*

I spy
six ducks

6

Utagawa Kuniyoshi, *Boat Trip in Winter*

I spy
seven circles

7

Wassily Kandinsky, *Swinging*

I spy
eight boats

Vincent Van Gogh, *Boats on the Beach*

I spy
nine children

9

Studio of Peter Paul Rubens, *The Gerbier Family*

I spy
ten hens

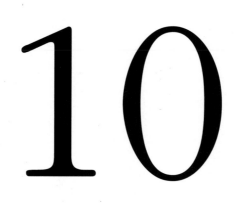

10

Sir Stanley Spencer, *St. Francis and the Birds*

I spy
eleven hares

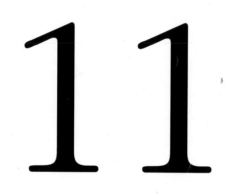

Unknown artist, *The Emblem of the Hare*

I spy
twelve squirrels

Abu'l Hasan, *Squirrels in a Plane Tree*

I spy
thirteen singers

Thomas Cooper Gotch, *Alleluia*

I spy
fourteen soldiers

14

Henri Rousseau, *Artillerymen*

I spy
fifteen hands and feet

15

Fernand Léger, *Divers on a Yellow Background*

I spy
sixteen apples

Lucas Cranach the Elder, *Madonna and Child under an Apple Tree*

I spy
seventeen birds

Pablo Picasso, *The New Year*

I spy
eighteen cherries

18

Georg Flegel, *Still Life*

I spy
nineteen stars

Robert Indiana, *The American Dream I* (1961)

I spy
twenty angels

Sandro Botticelli, *Mystic Nativity*

I Spied Numbers in Art...

1 one fly
Swabian School (15th century),
Portrait of a Woman of the Hofer Family
The National Gallery, London

2 two eyes
Karel Appel (born 1921), *Cry for Freedom* (1948)
Stedelijk Museum, Amsterdam

3 three puppies
Paul Gauguin (1848–1903), *Still Life with Three Puppies* (1888)
The Museum of Modern Art, New York, Mrs. Simon Guggenheim Fund

4 four fish
Henri Matisse (1869–1954), *Goldfish* (1911)
Pushkin Museum, Moscow

5 five eggs
Jan van Huijsum (1682–1749),
Flowers in a Terracotta Vase (1736–1737)
The National Gallery, London

6 six ducks
Utagawa Kuniyoshi (1797–1861), *Boat Trip in Winter* (about 1853)
Van Gogh Museum, Amsterdam

7 seven circles
Wassily Kandinsky (1866–1944), *Swinging* (1925)
The Tate Gallery, London

8 eight boats

Vincent Van Gogh (1853–1890), *Boats on the Beach* (1888)
Van Gogh Museum, Amsterdam

9 nine children

Studio of Peter Paul Rubens (1577–1640),
The Gerbier Family (about 1630)
The Royal Collection, St. James's Palace, London

10 ten hens

Sir Stanley Spencer (1891–1959), *St. Francis and the Birds* (1935)
The Tate Gallery, London

11 eleven hares

Unknown artist, *The Emblem of the Hare*
from *Le Livre de la Chasse* (about 1405–1410) by Gaston Phébus
Bibliotèque Nationale, Paris

12 twelve squirrels

Abu'l Hasan (17th century), *Squirrels in a Plane Tree* (about 1610)
The British Library, London

13 thirteen singers

Thomas Cooper Gotch (1854–1931), *Alleluia* (exhibited 1896)
The Tate Gallery, London

14 fourteen soldiers

Henri Rousseau (1844–1910), *Artillerymen* (about 1893–1895)
The Solomon R. Guggenheim Museum, New York,
Gift of Solomon R. Guggenheim

15 fifteen hands and feet

Fernand Léger (1881–1955),
Divers on a Yellow Background (1941)
The Art Institute of Chicago, Gift of Mr. and Mrs. Maurice Culberg

16 sixteen apples

Lucas Cranach the Elder (1472–1553),
Madonna and Child under an Apple Tree
Hermitage Museum, St. Petersburg

17 seventeen birds

Pablo Picasso (1881–1973), *The New Year* (1953)
Saint-Denis Musée d'Art et d'Histoire, Paris

18 eighteen cherries

Georg Flegel (1566–1638), *Still Life*
Private Collection

19 nineteen stars

Robert Indiana (born 1928), *The American Dream I* (1961)
The Museum of Modern Art, New York, Gift of The Larry Aldrich Foundation Fund

20 twenty angels

Sandro Botticelli (about 1445–1510), *Mystic Nativity* (1500)
The National Gallery, London

ACKNOWLEDGMENTS

The author and publishers would like to thank the galleries, museums, private collectors, and copyright holders who have given their permission to reproduce the pictures in this book.

Swabian School, *Portrait of a Woman of the Hofer Family;*
Jan van Huijsum, *Flowers in a Terracotta Vase;*
Sandro Botticelli, *Mystic Nativity,*
The Trustees, The National Gallery, London.

Karel Appel, *Cry for Freedom* © Karel Appel
c/o De Tulp Pers 1993/N.V. Koninklijk Bijenkorf Beheer.

Paul Gauguin, *Still Life with Three Puppies,* oil on wood, 91.8 x 62.6 cm.,
photograph © 1992 The Museum of Modern Art, New York.

Henri Matisse, *Goldfish* © Succession H. Matisse/D.A.C.S. 1993,
photograph: Bridgeman Art Library, London.

Utagawa Kuniyoshi, *Boat Trip in Winter;*
Vincent Van Gogh, *Boats on the Beach,*
Vincent Van Gogh Foundation/Van Gogh Museum, Amsterdam.

Wassily Kandinsky, *Swinging*
© A.D.A.G.P., Paris and D.A.C.S., London 1993.

Studio of Peter Paul Rubens, *The Gerbier Family* © H. M. The Queen.

Sir Stanley Spencer, *St. Francis and the Birds*
© Estate of Stanley Spencer 1993, all rights reserved D.A.C.S.

Abu'l Hasan, *Squirrels in a Plane Tree,* by permission of the British Library.

Thomas Cooper Gotch, *Alleluia,* photograph: John Webb.

Henri Rousseau, *Artillerymen,* photograph: David Heald
© The Solomon R. Guggenheim Foundation, New York, 1993.

Fernand Léger, French, *Divers on a Yellow Background,*
photograph courtesy of The Art Institute of Chicago/© D.A.C.S. 1993.

Lucas Cranach the Elder, *Madonna and Child under an Apple Tree,*
photograph: Bridgeman Art Library, London.

Pablo Picasso, *The New Year* © D.A.C.S. 1993.

Georg Flegel, *Still Life* © Christie's 1993.

Robert Indiana, *The American Dream I,* oil on canvas, 183 x 152.7 cm.,
photograph © 1992 The Museum of Modern Art, New York.

Cover picture: Karel Appel, *Cry for Freedom* (1948)
Title page picture: Henri Rousseau, *Artillerymen* (about 1893-1895)

Compilation and text copyright © 1993 by Lucy Micklethwait
The author asserts the moral right to be identified as the author of the work.
First published in Great Britain in 1993 by HarperCollins Publishers Ltd.
First published in the United States in 1993 by Greenwillow Books.
All rights reserved. No part of this book may be reproduced or utilized in
any form or by any means, electronic or mechanical, including photocopying,
recording, or by any information storage and retrieval system, without
permission in writing from the Publisher, Greenwillow Books, a division of
William Morrow & Company, Inc., 1350 Avenue of the Americas, New York, NY 10019.
Printed in Great Britain
First American Edition   10 9 8 7 6 5 4 3 2 1

Library of Congress Cataloging-in-Publication Data
Micklethwait, Lucy.
I spy two eyes : numbers in art /
devised and selected by Lucy Micklethwait.
p.   cm.
Summary: Uses the subjects of well-known paintings
to introduce the numbers from one to twenty.
ISBN 0-688-12640-5 (trade).
ISBN 0-688-12642-1 (lib. bdg.)
1. Counting — Juvenile literature.
[1. Counting.   2. Art appreciation.]   I. Title.
QA113.M5   1993
513.2'11 — dc20   [E]
92-35641   CIP   AC